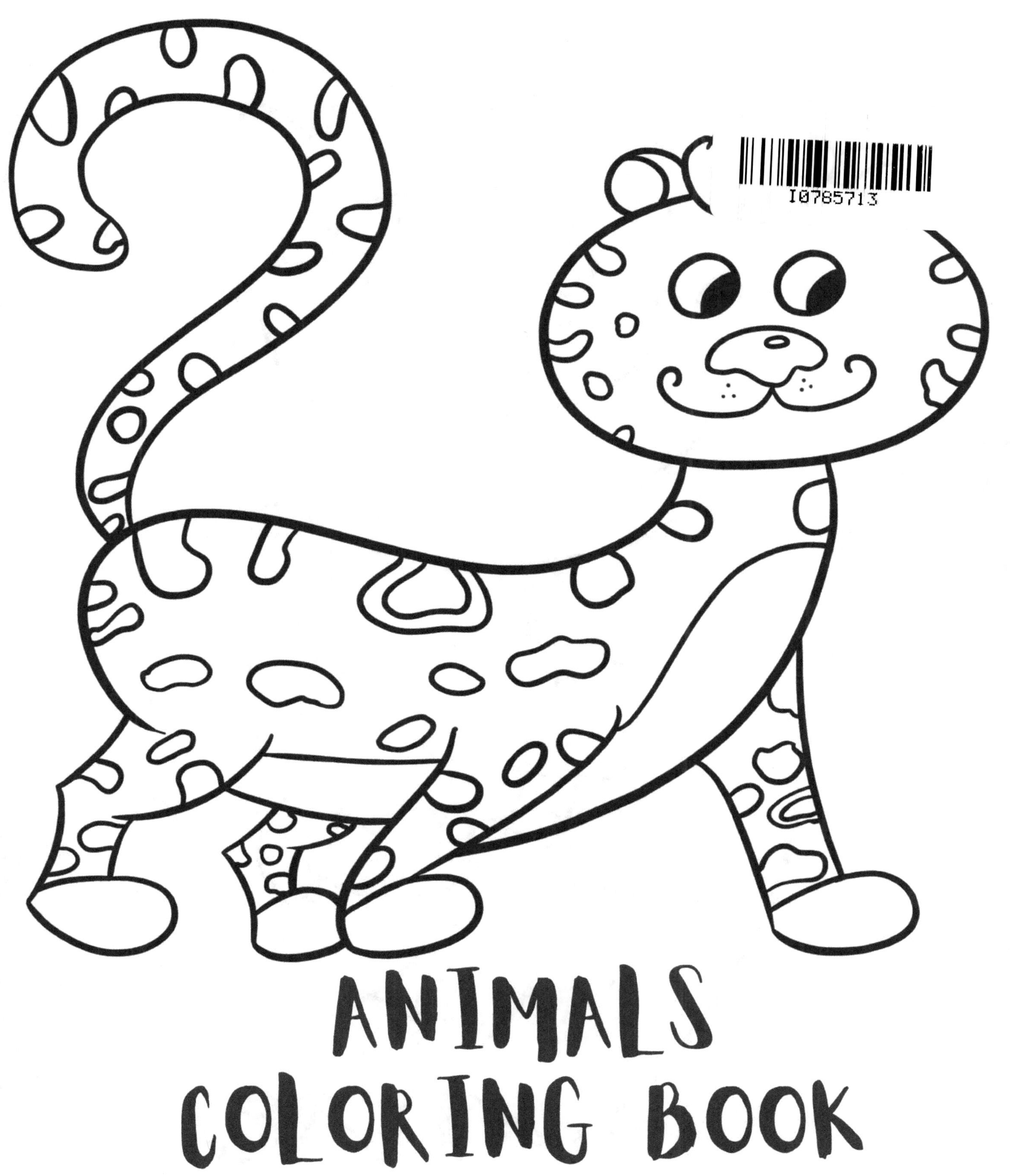

ANIMALS COLORING BOOK

HOLZ | 2018

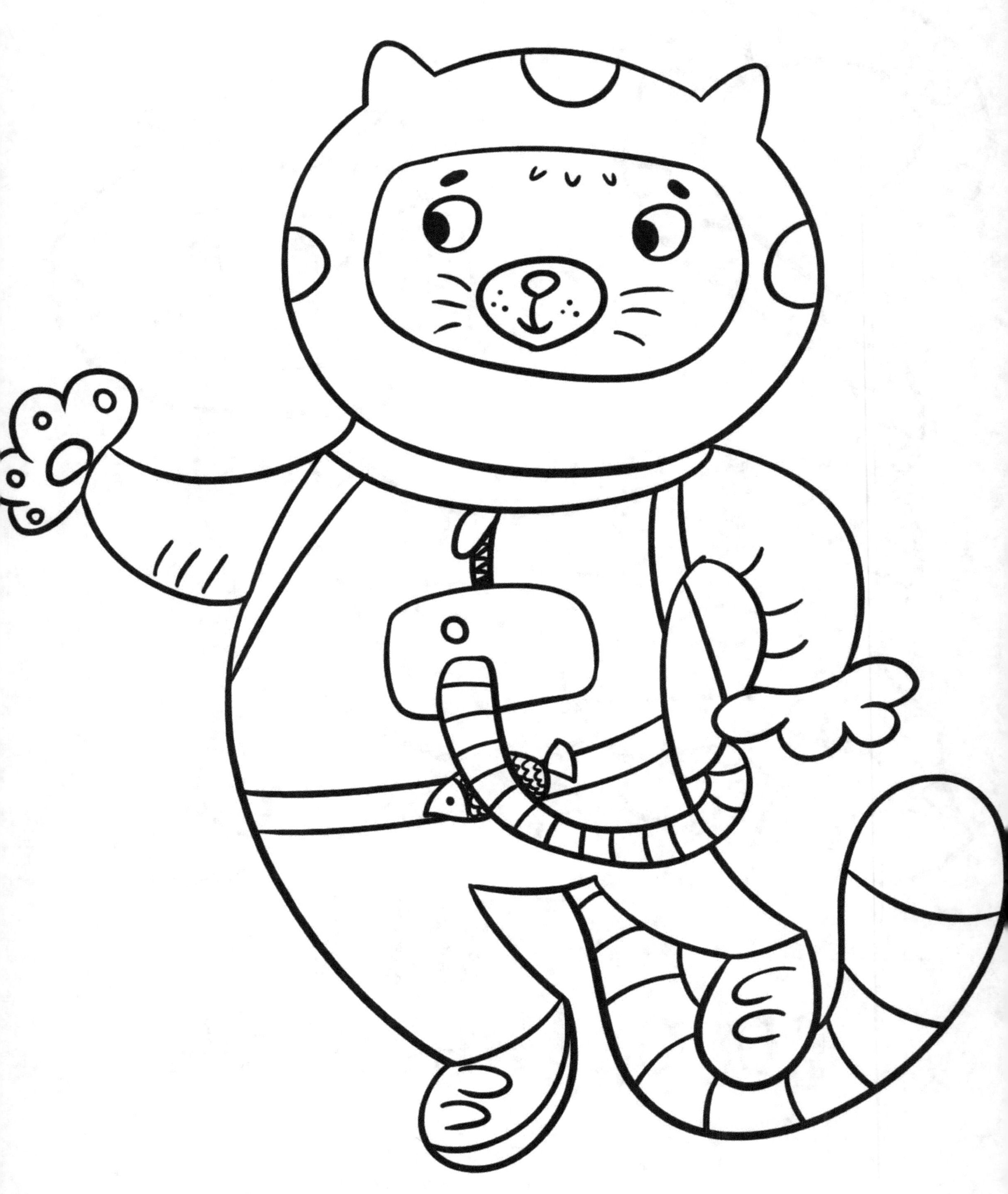

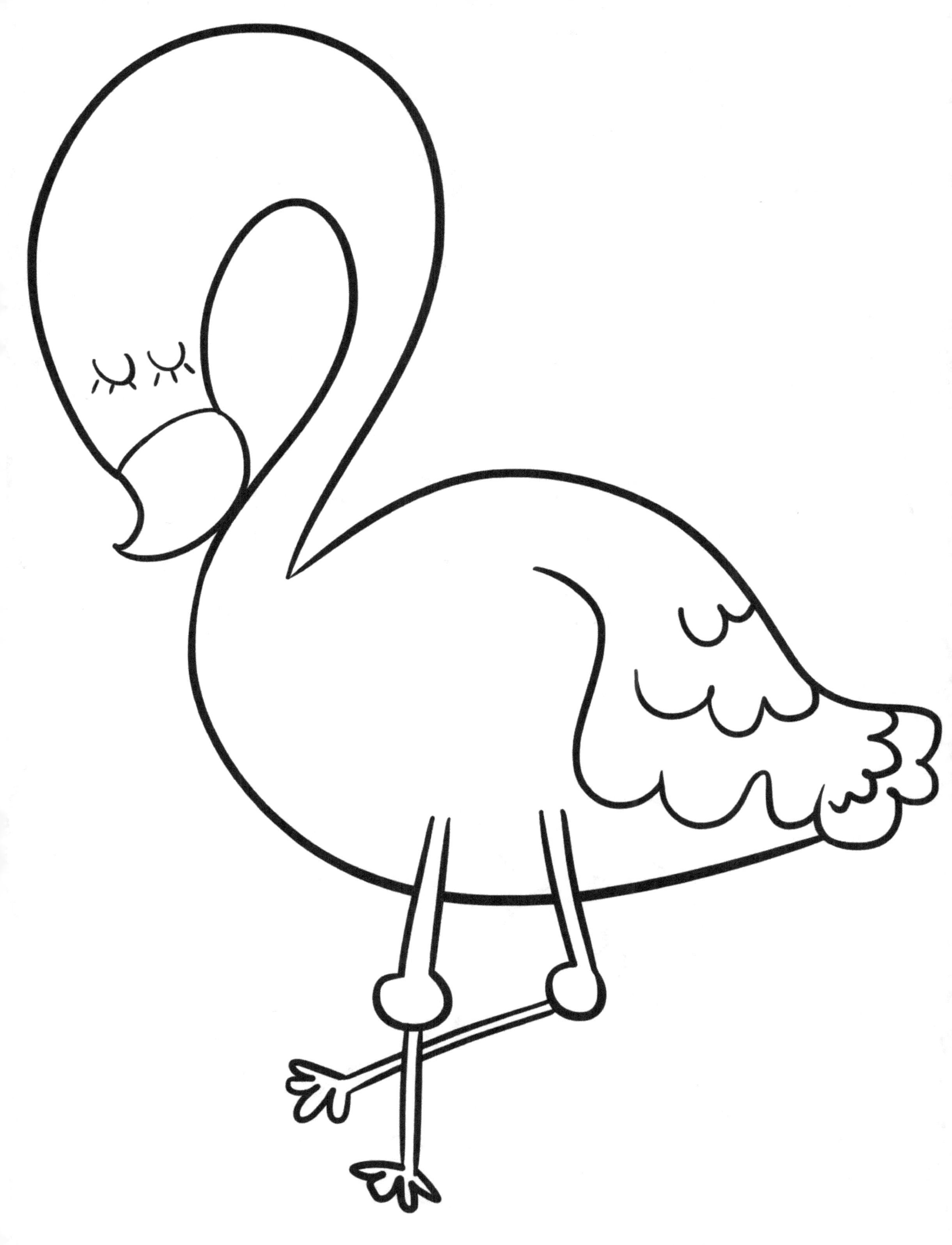

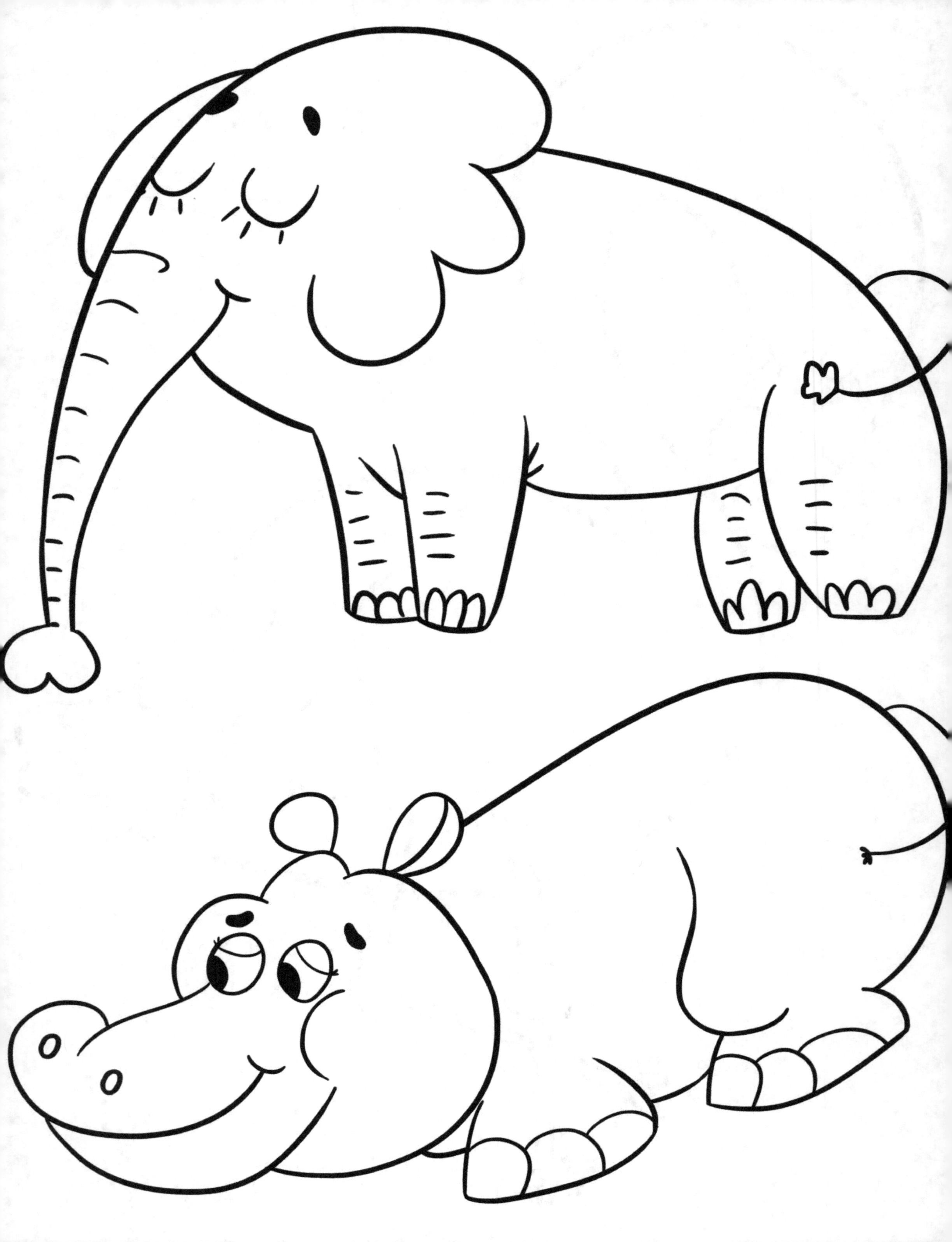

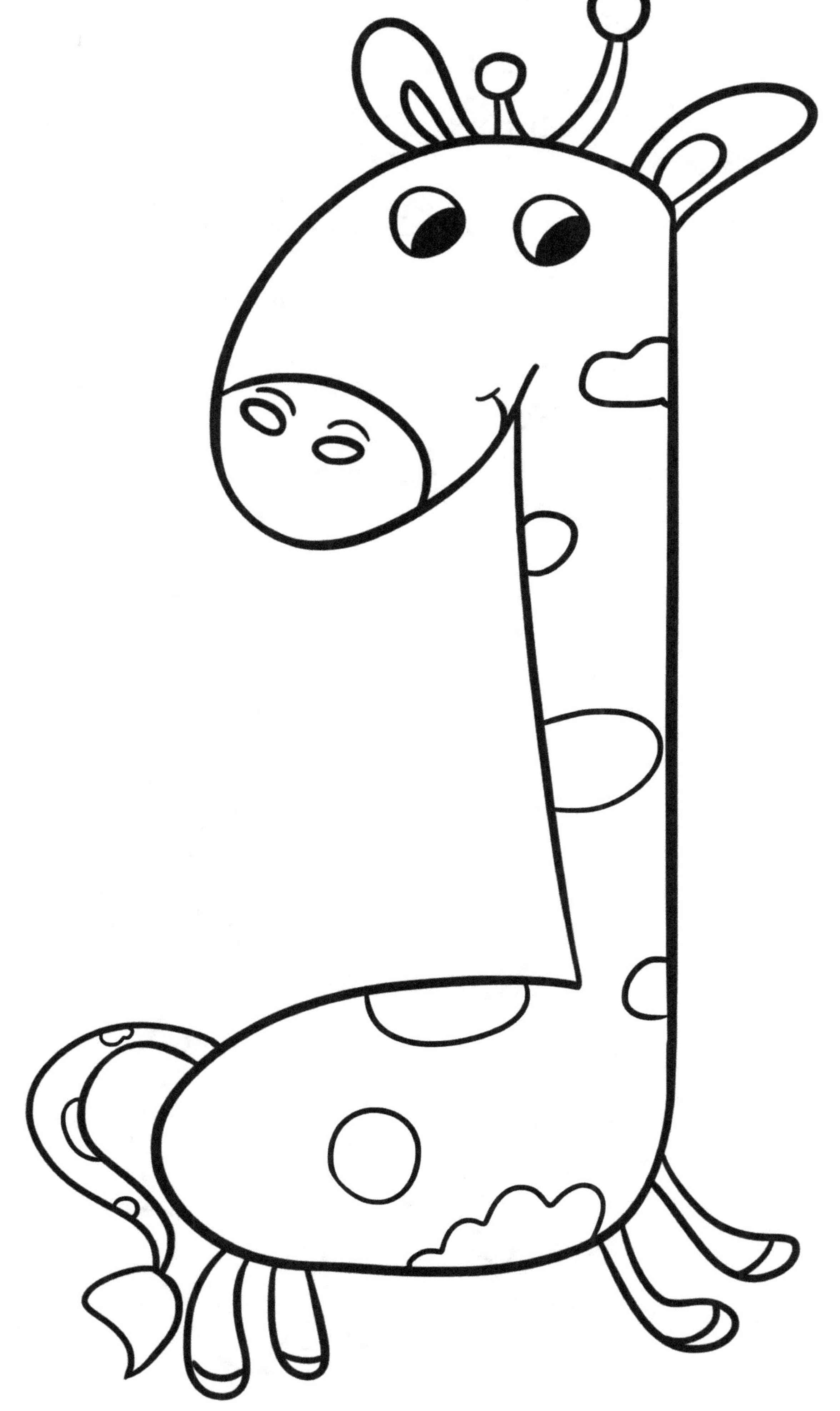

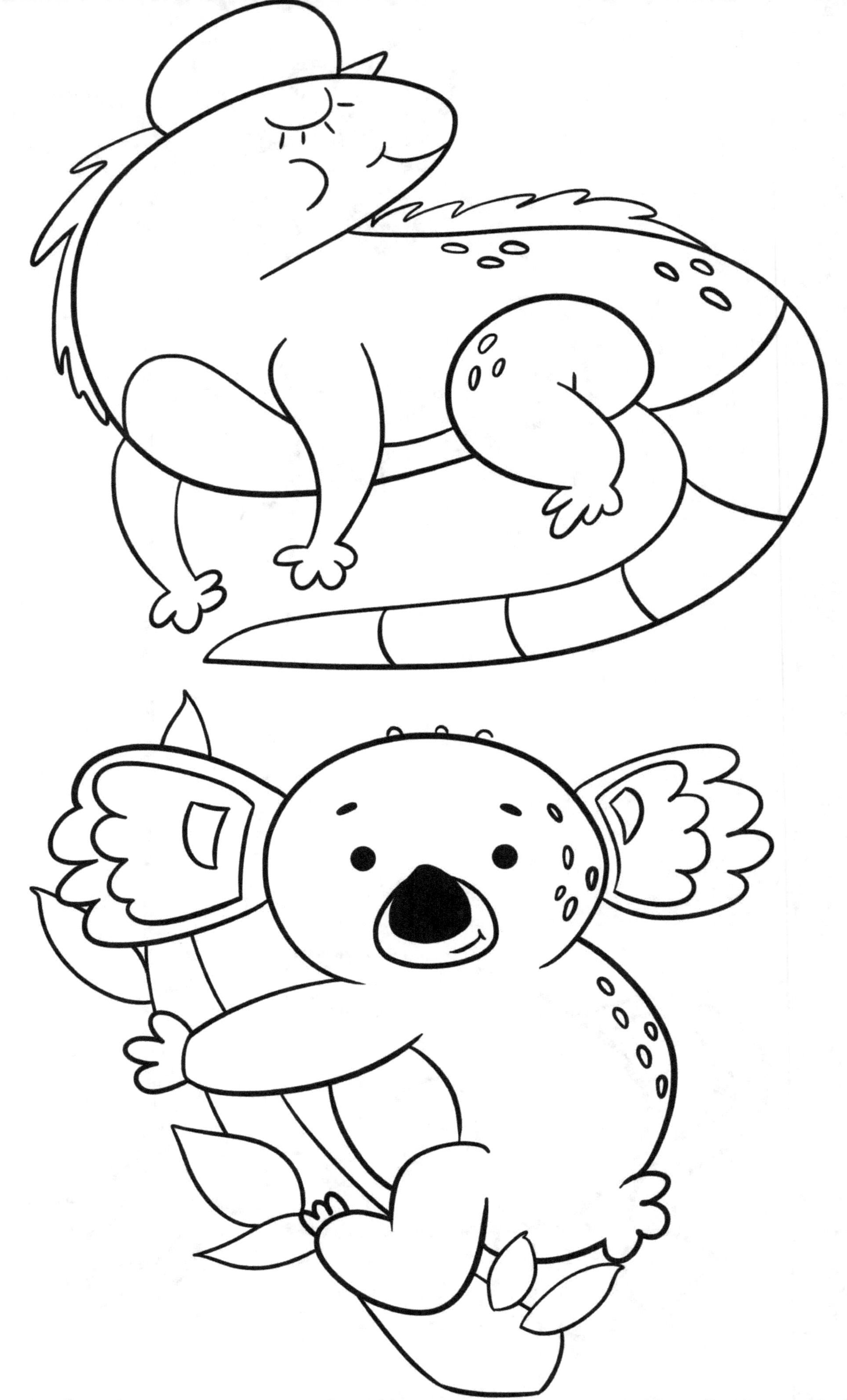

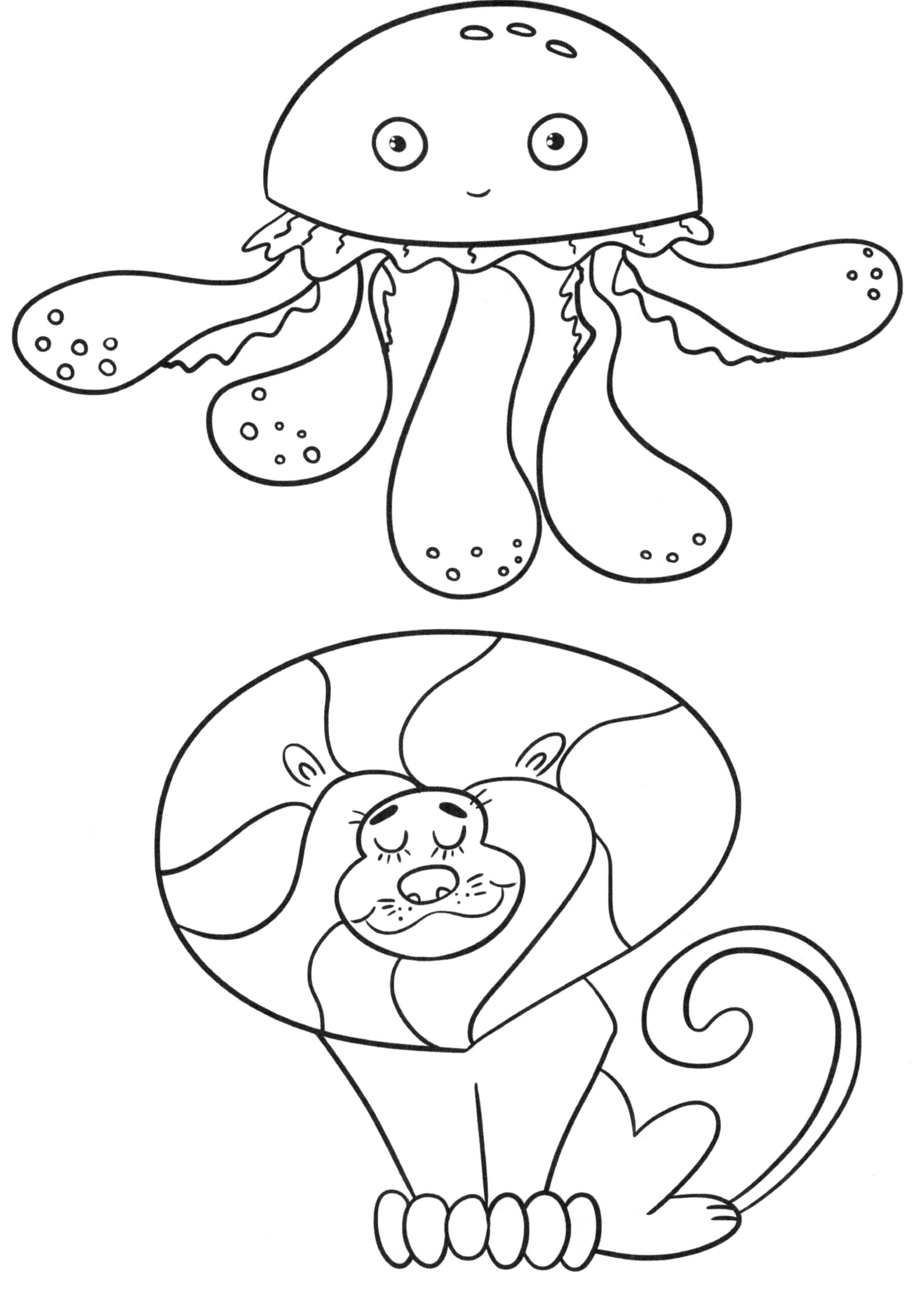

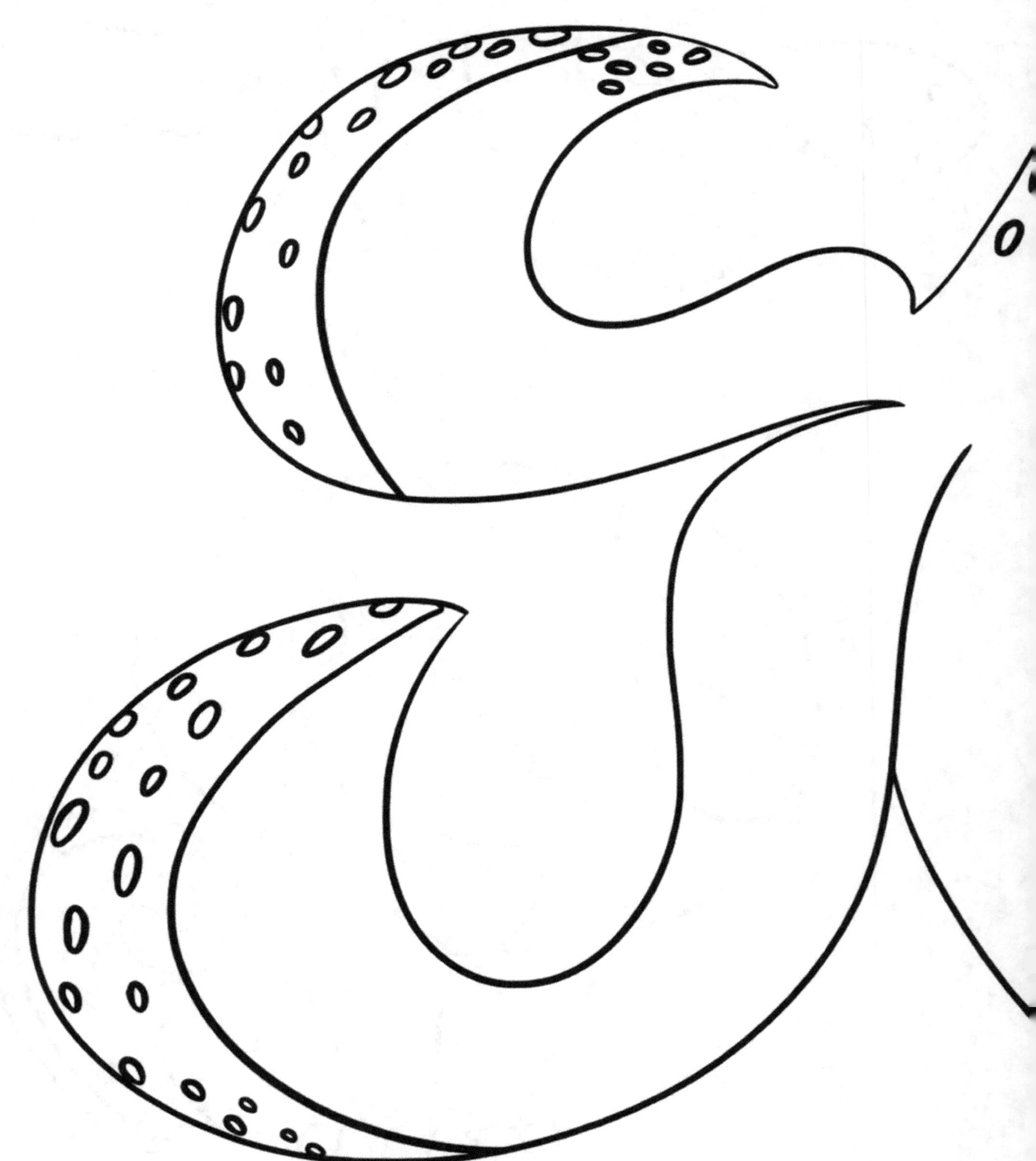

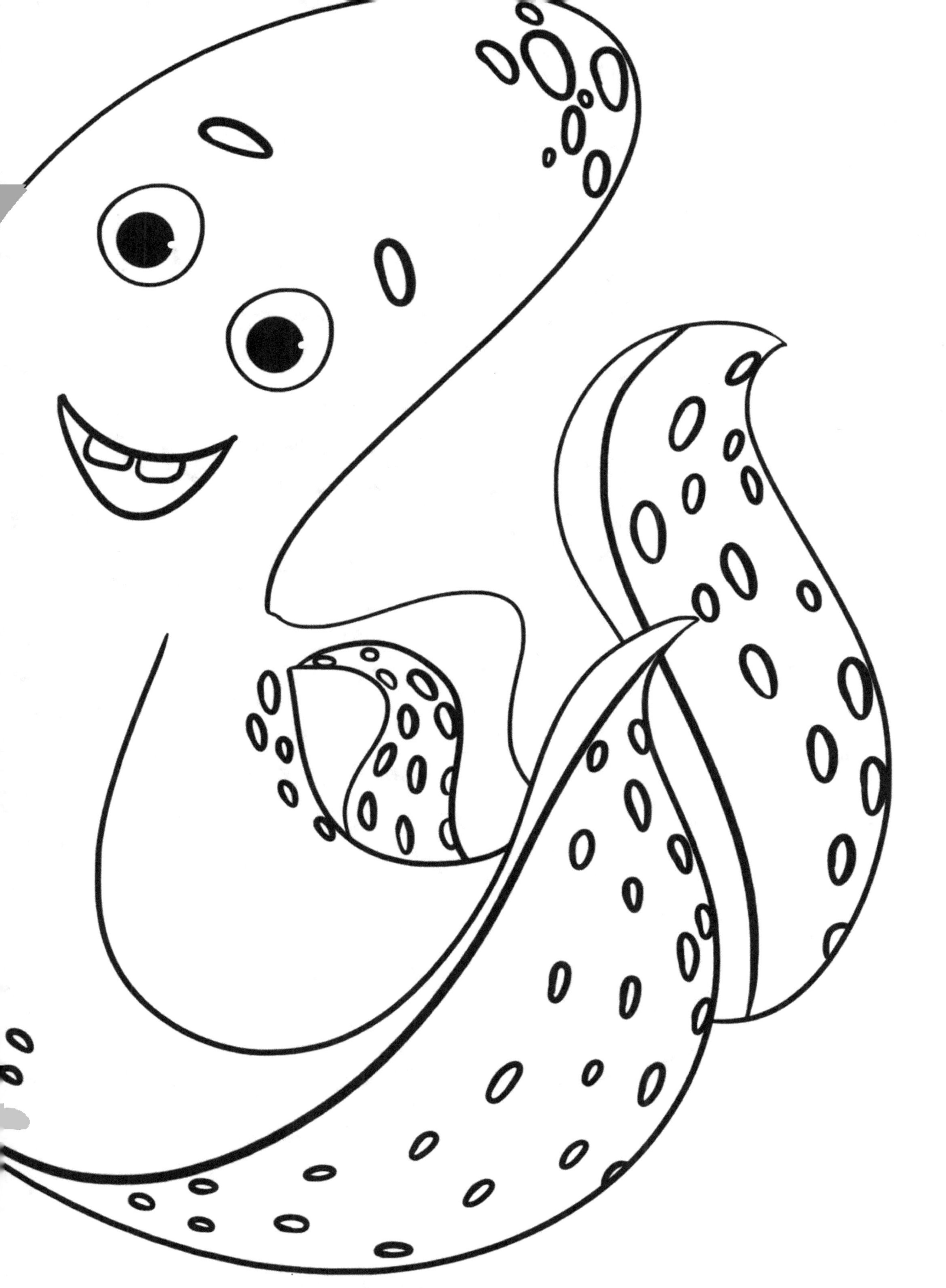

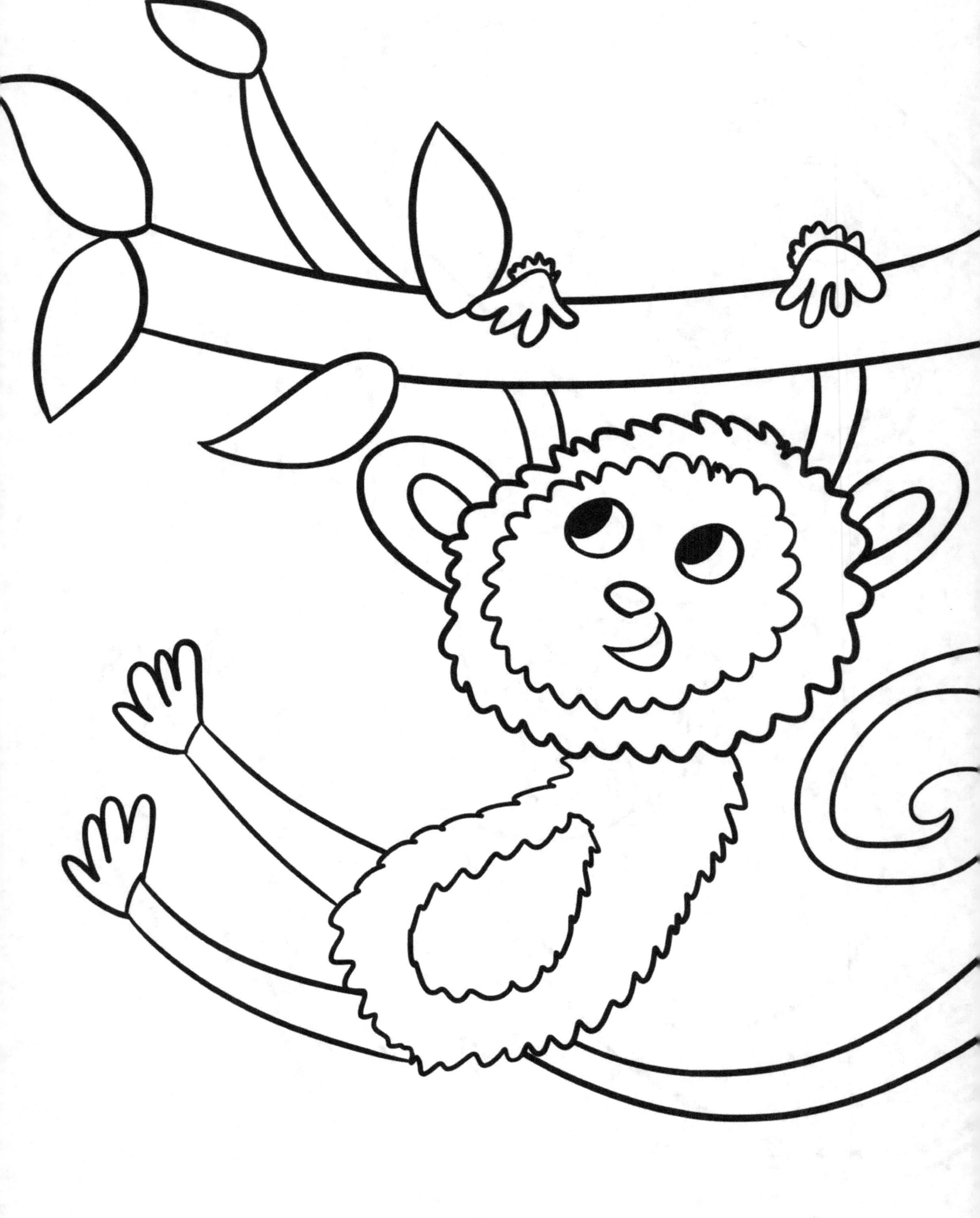

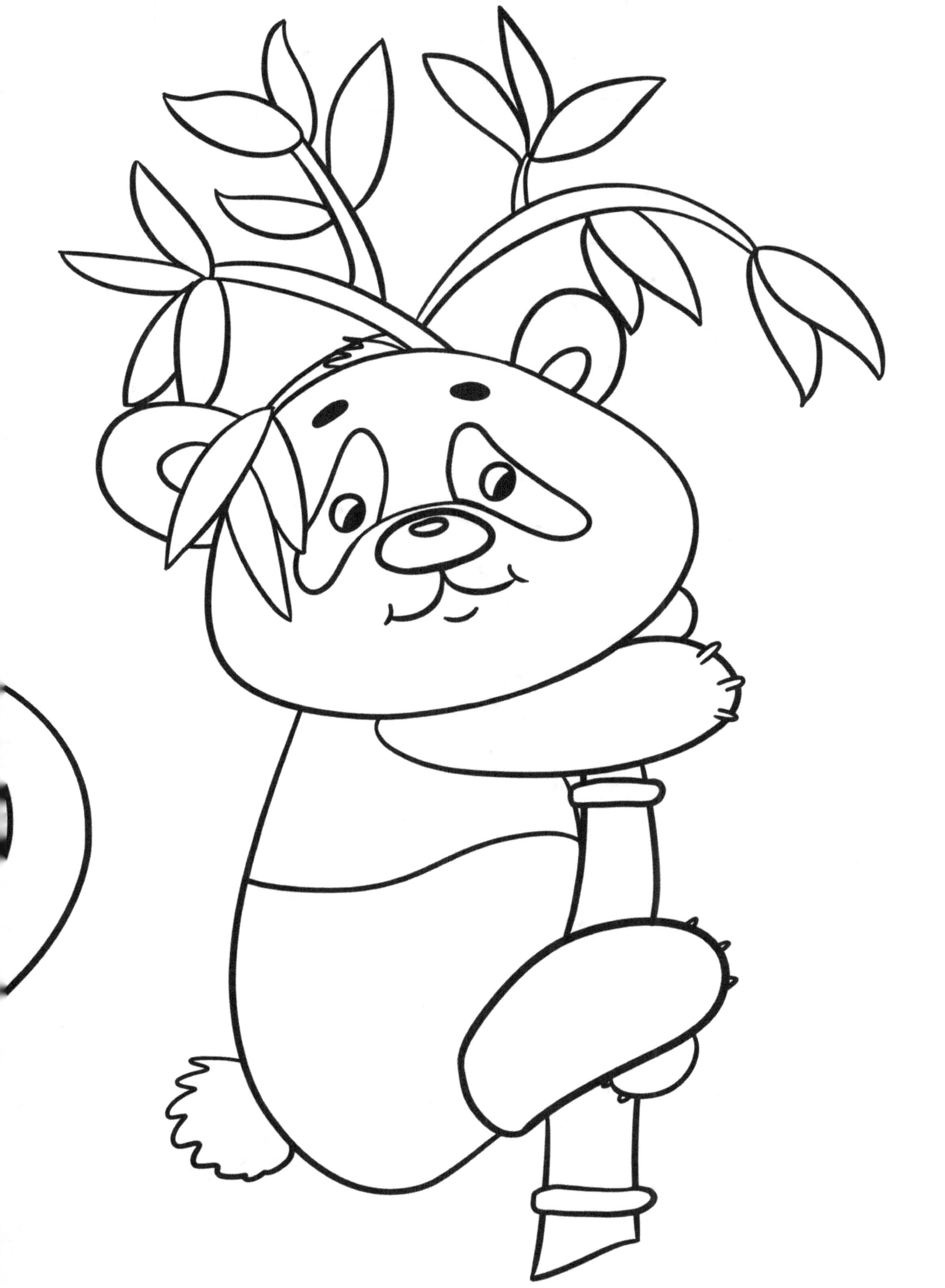

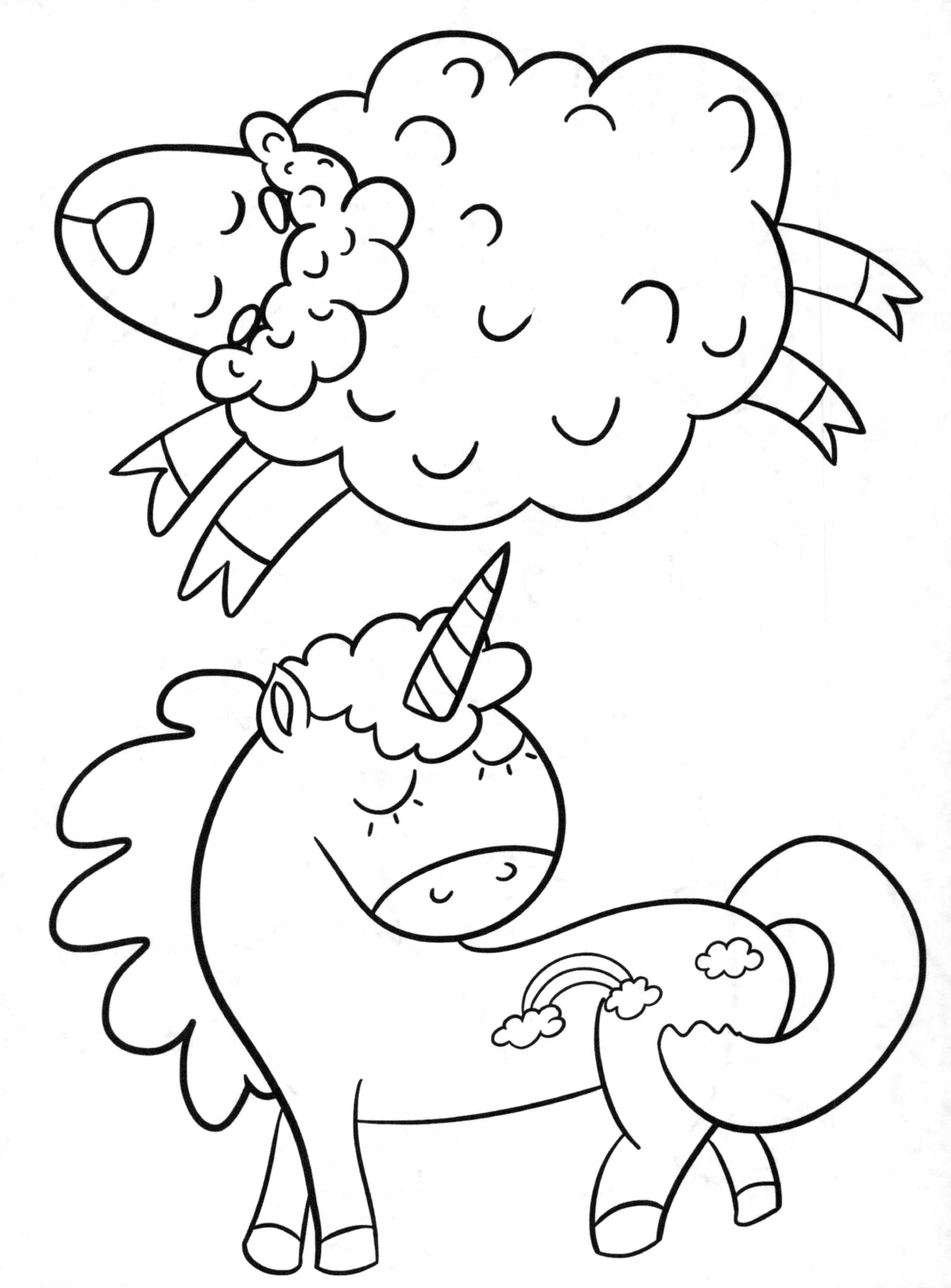

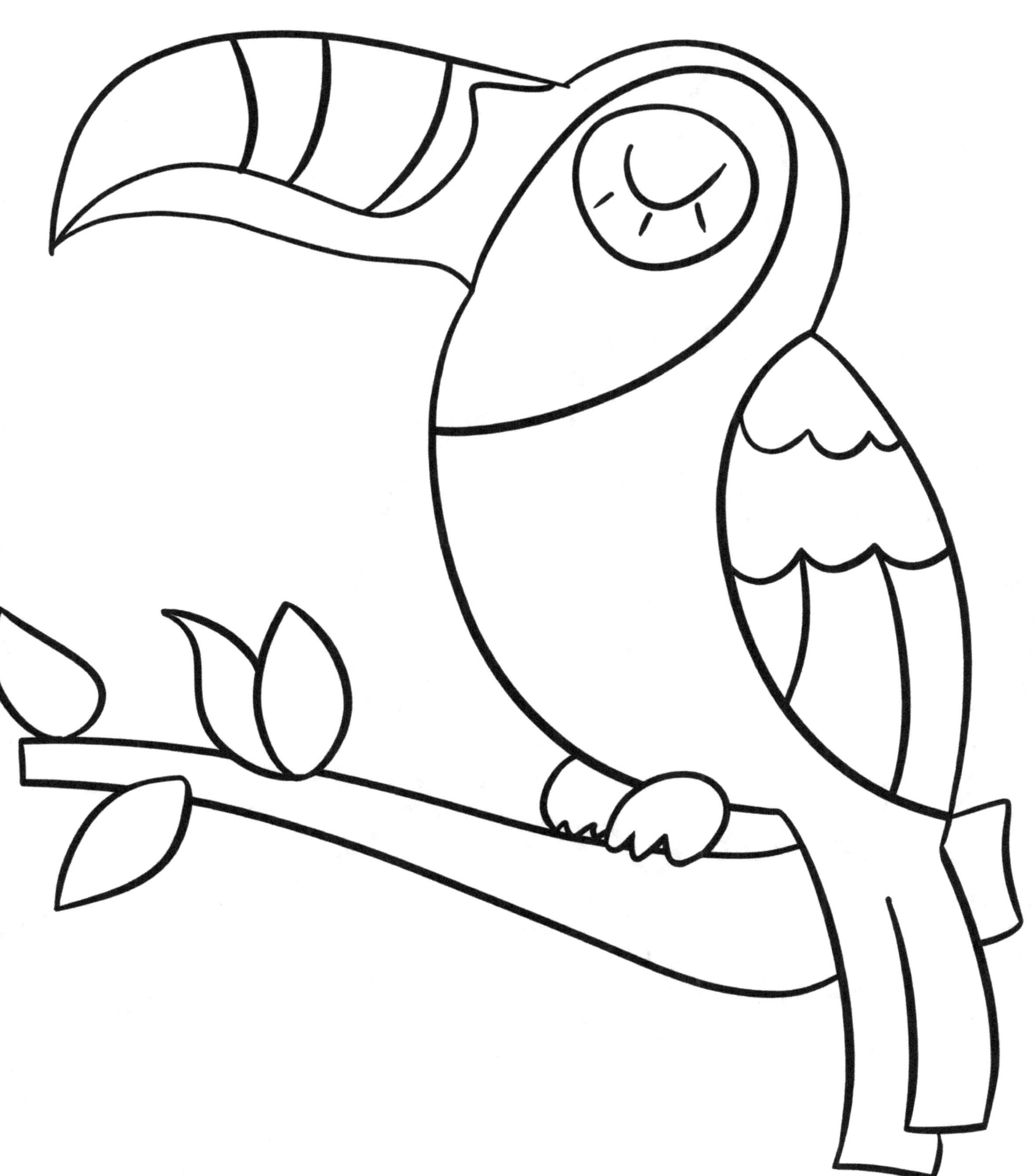

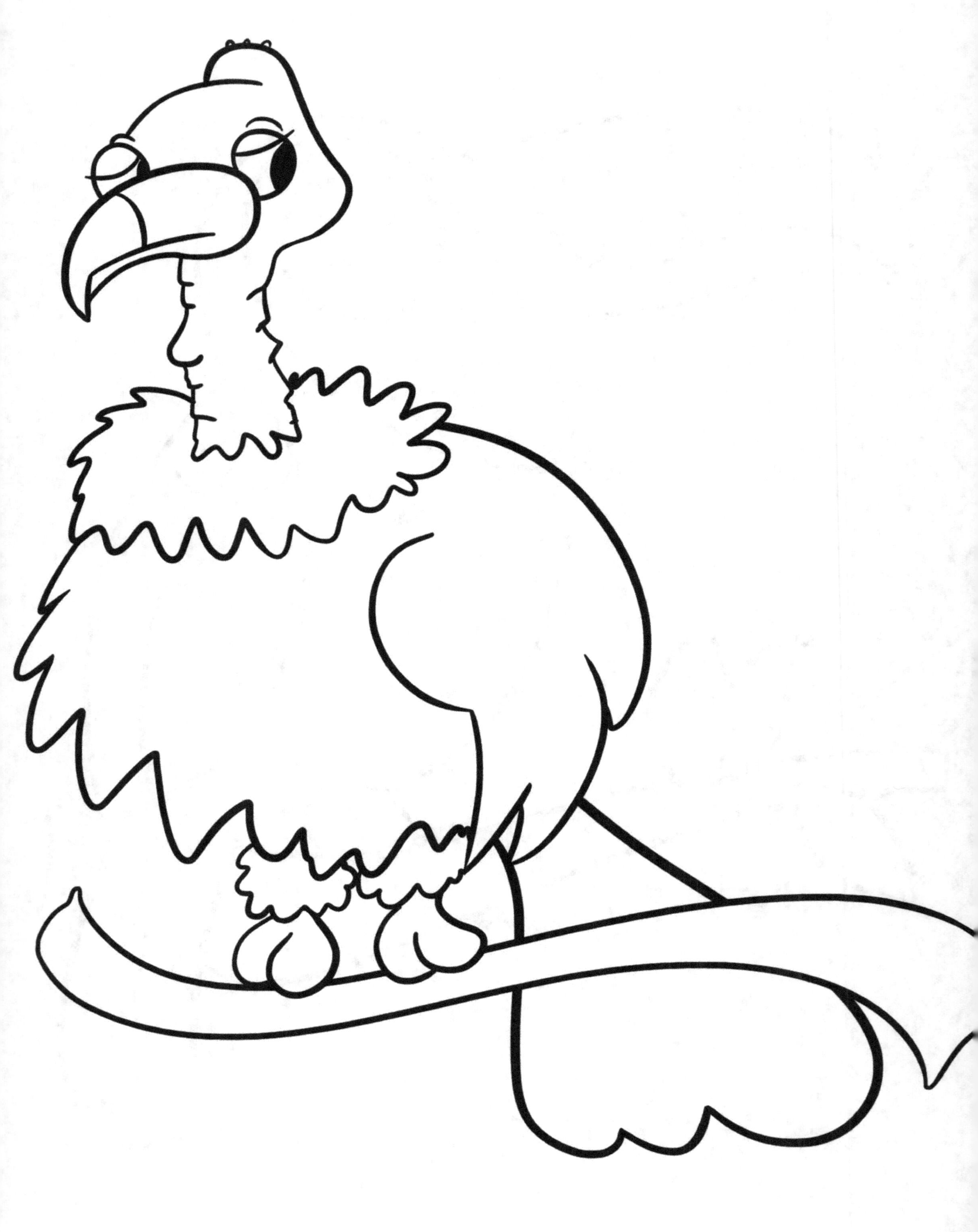

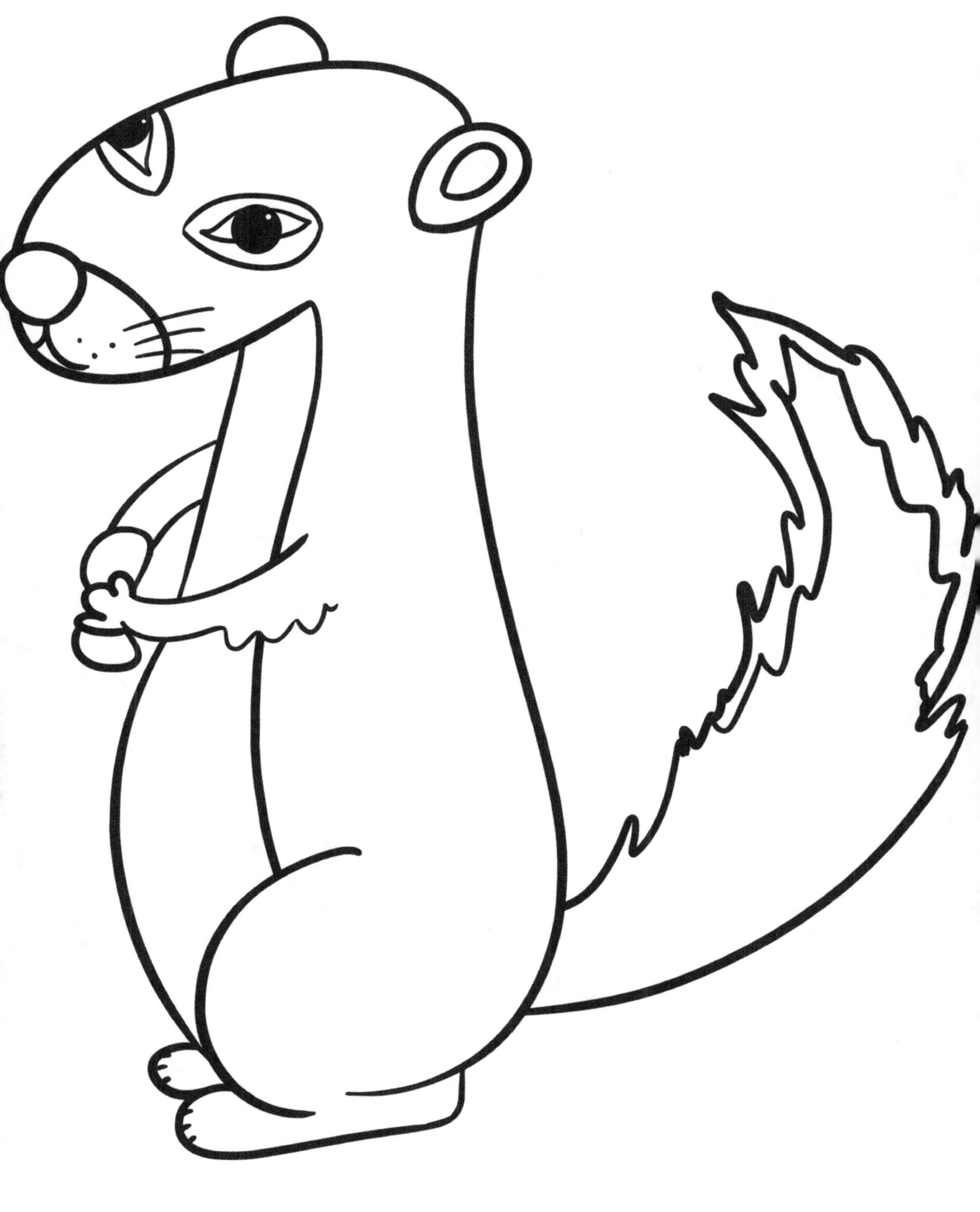

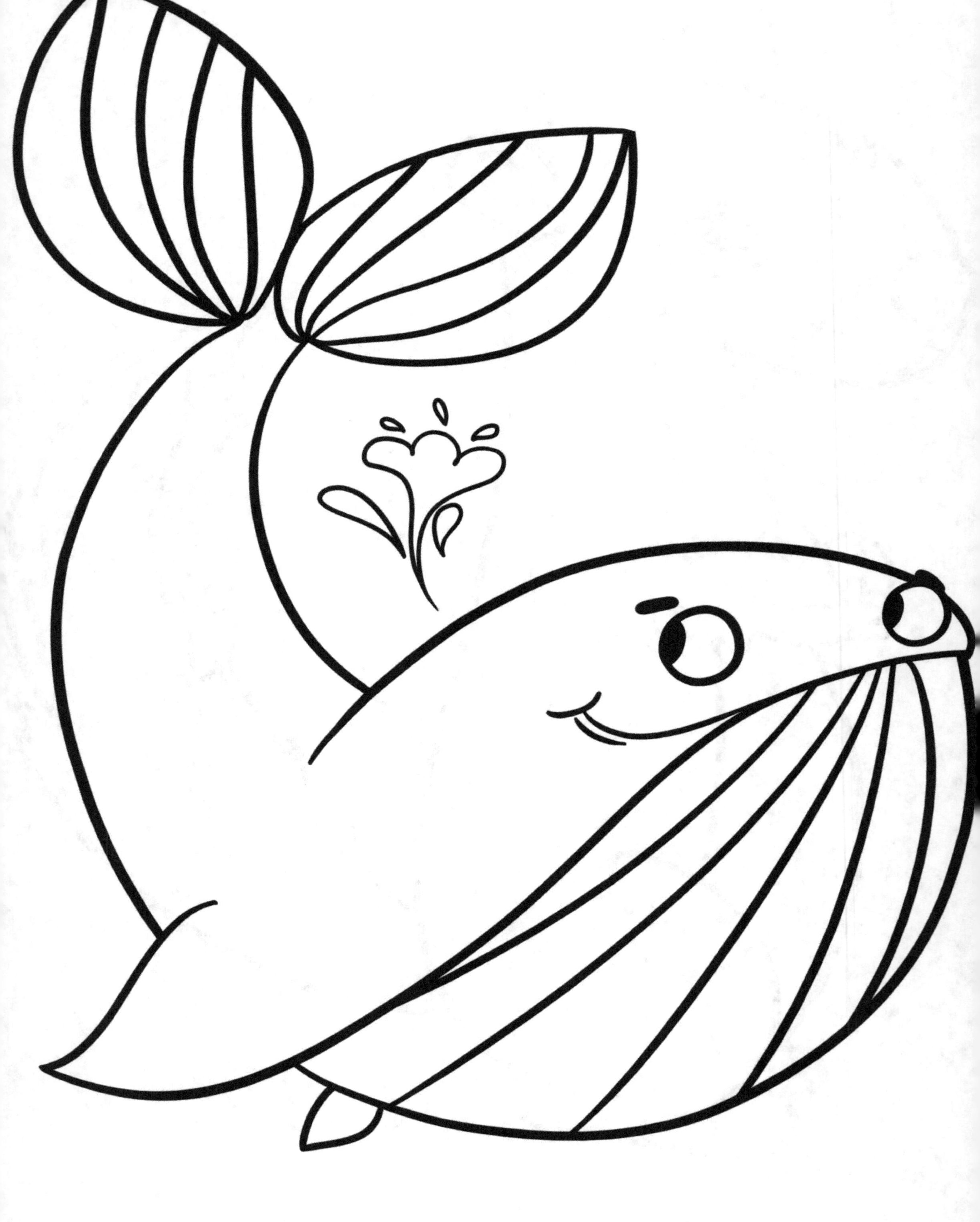

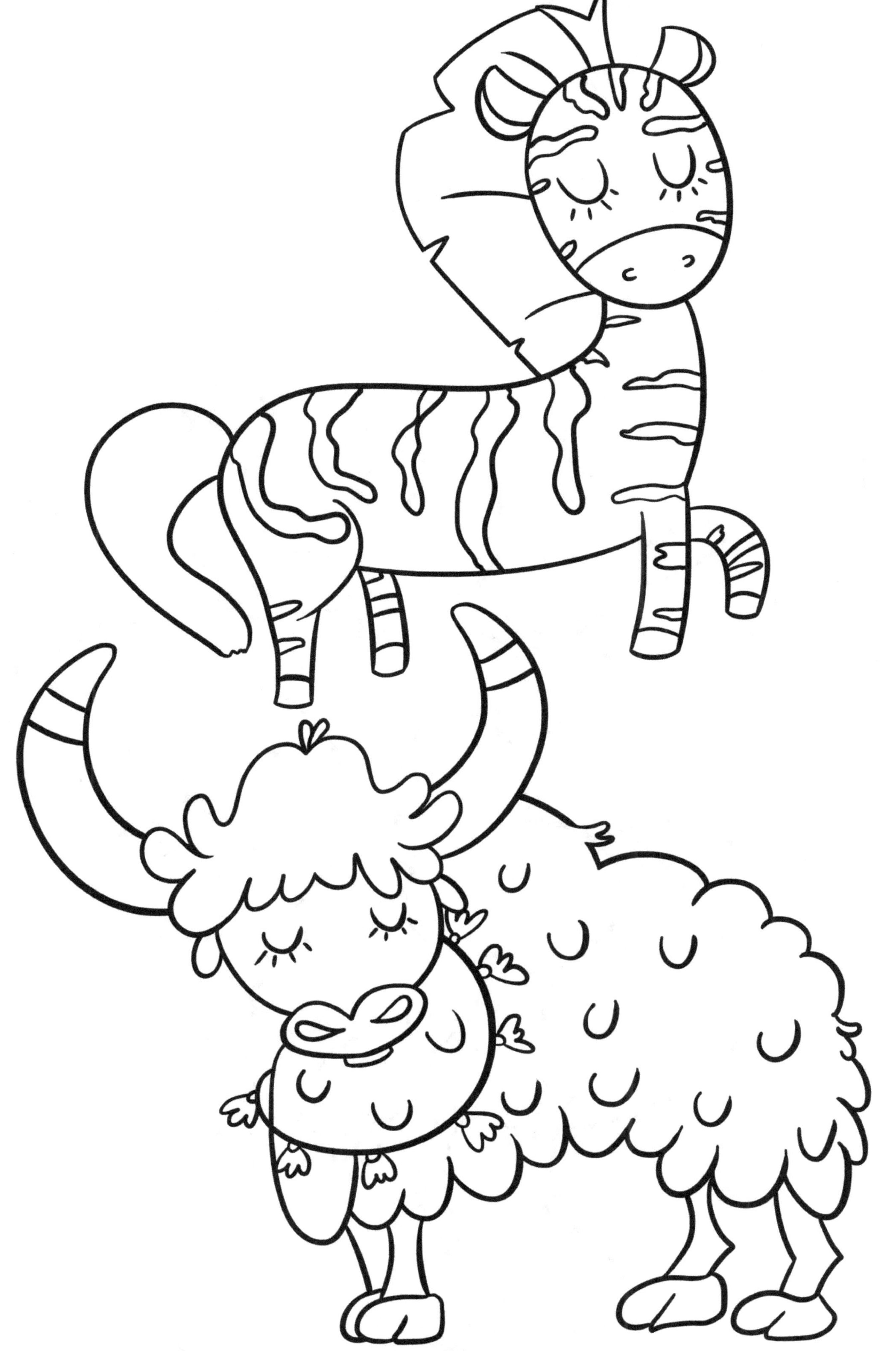

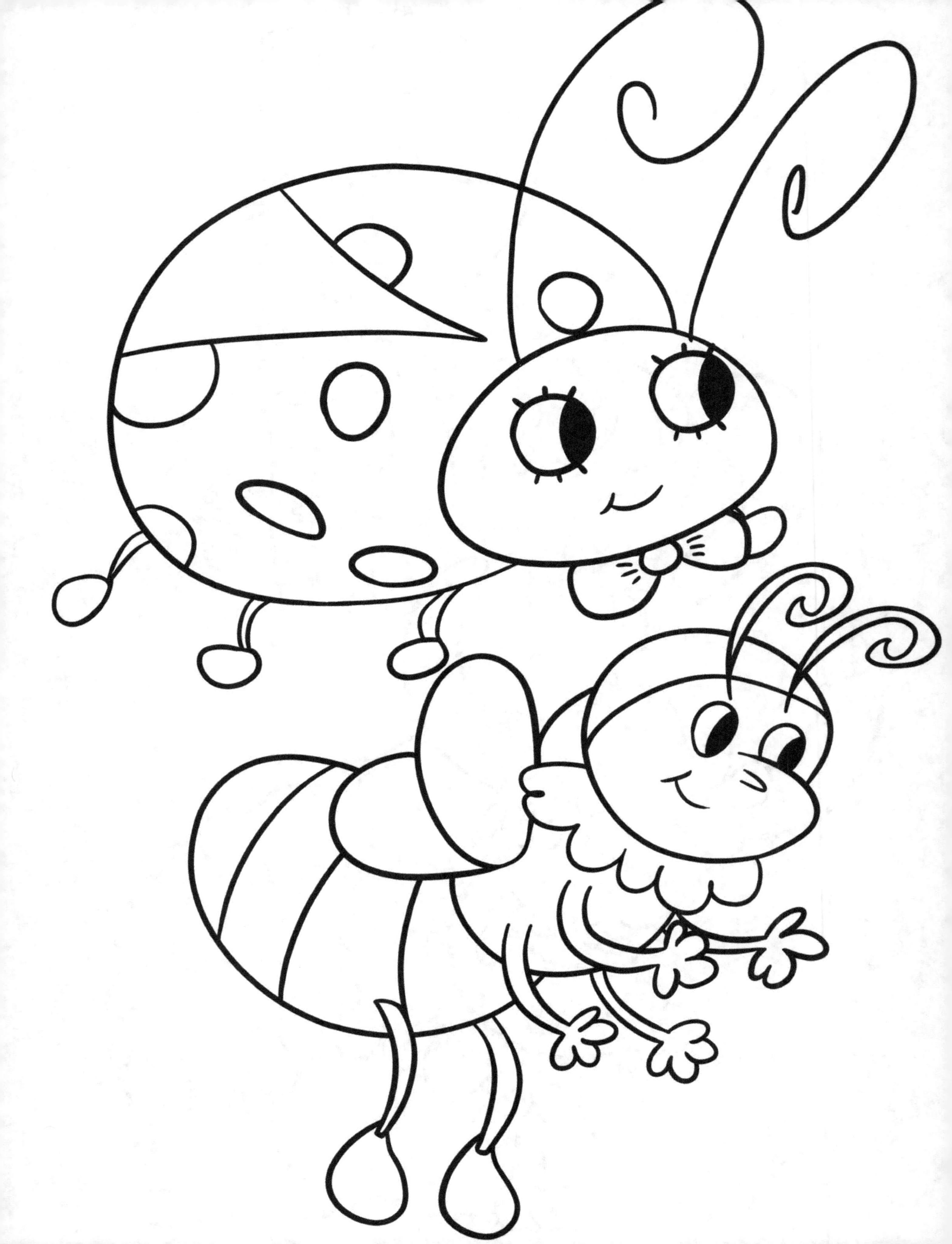

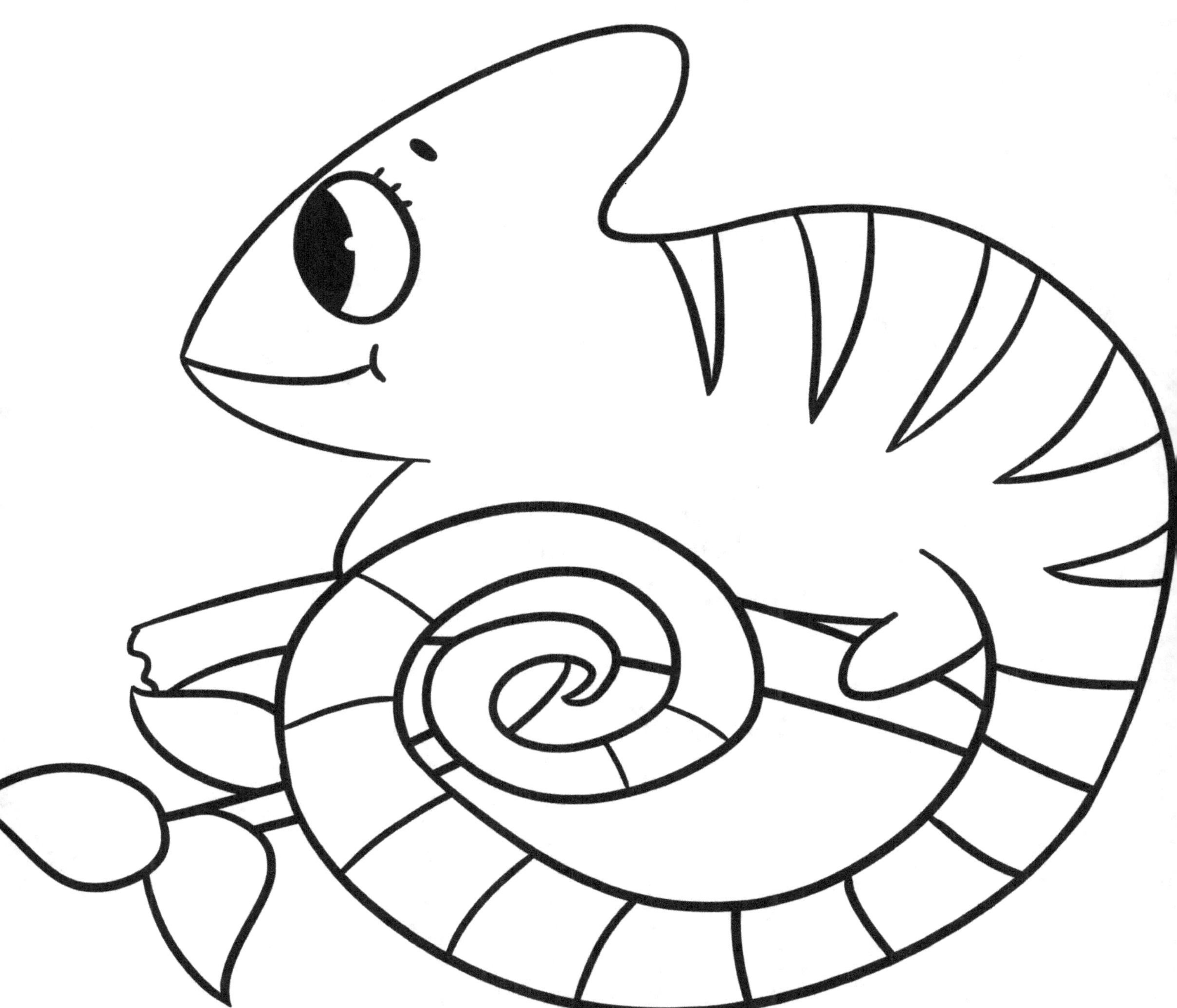

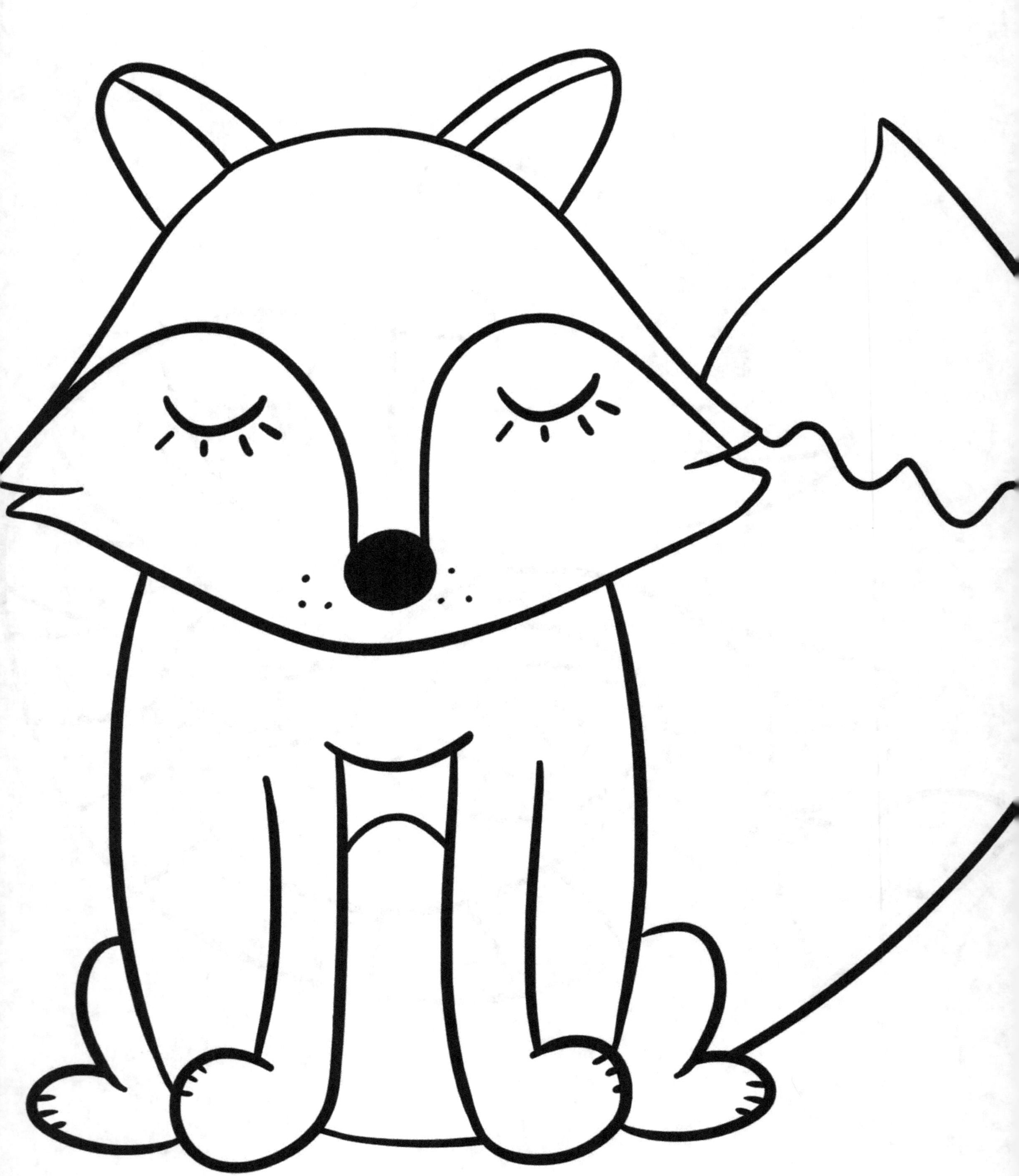

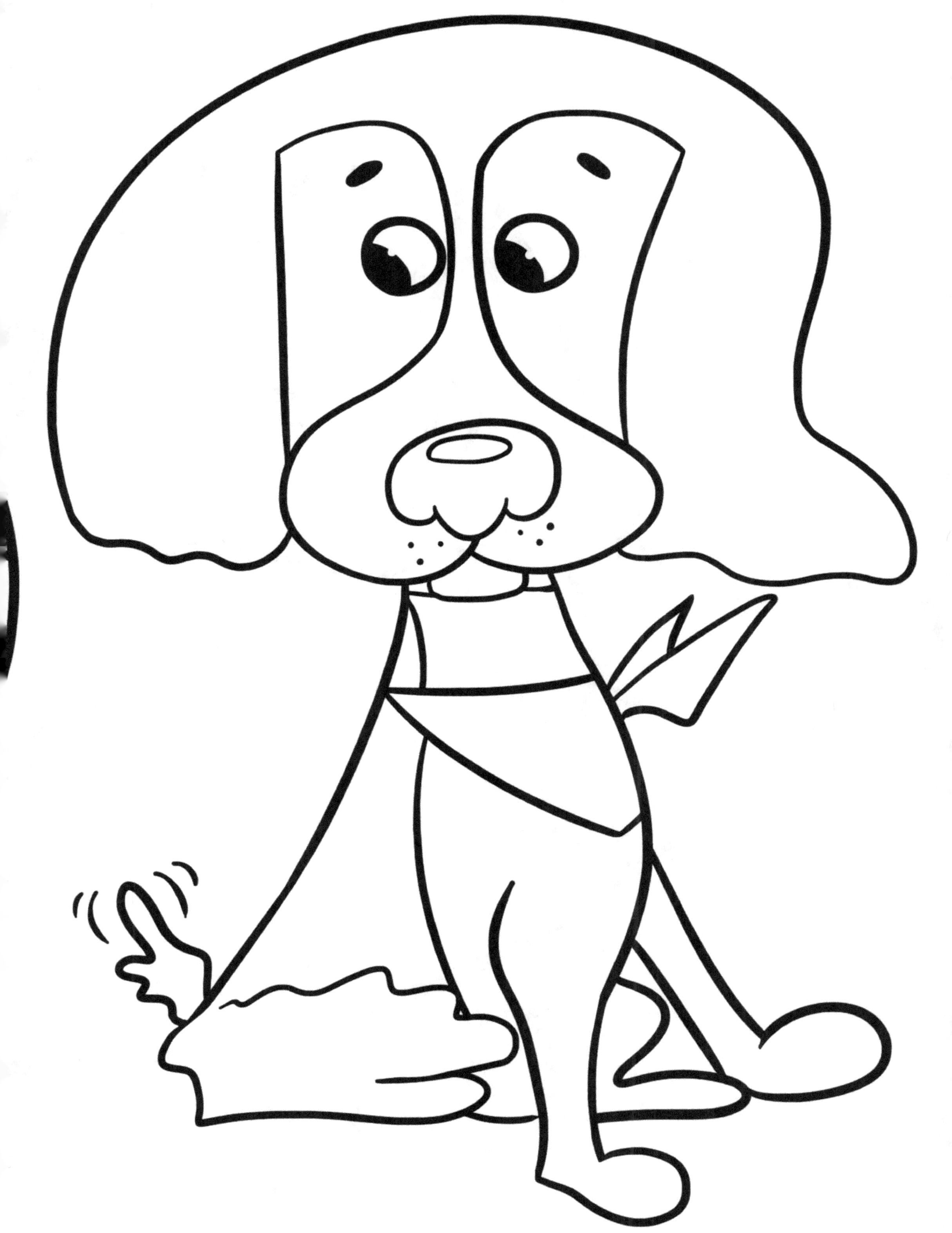

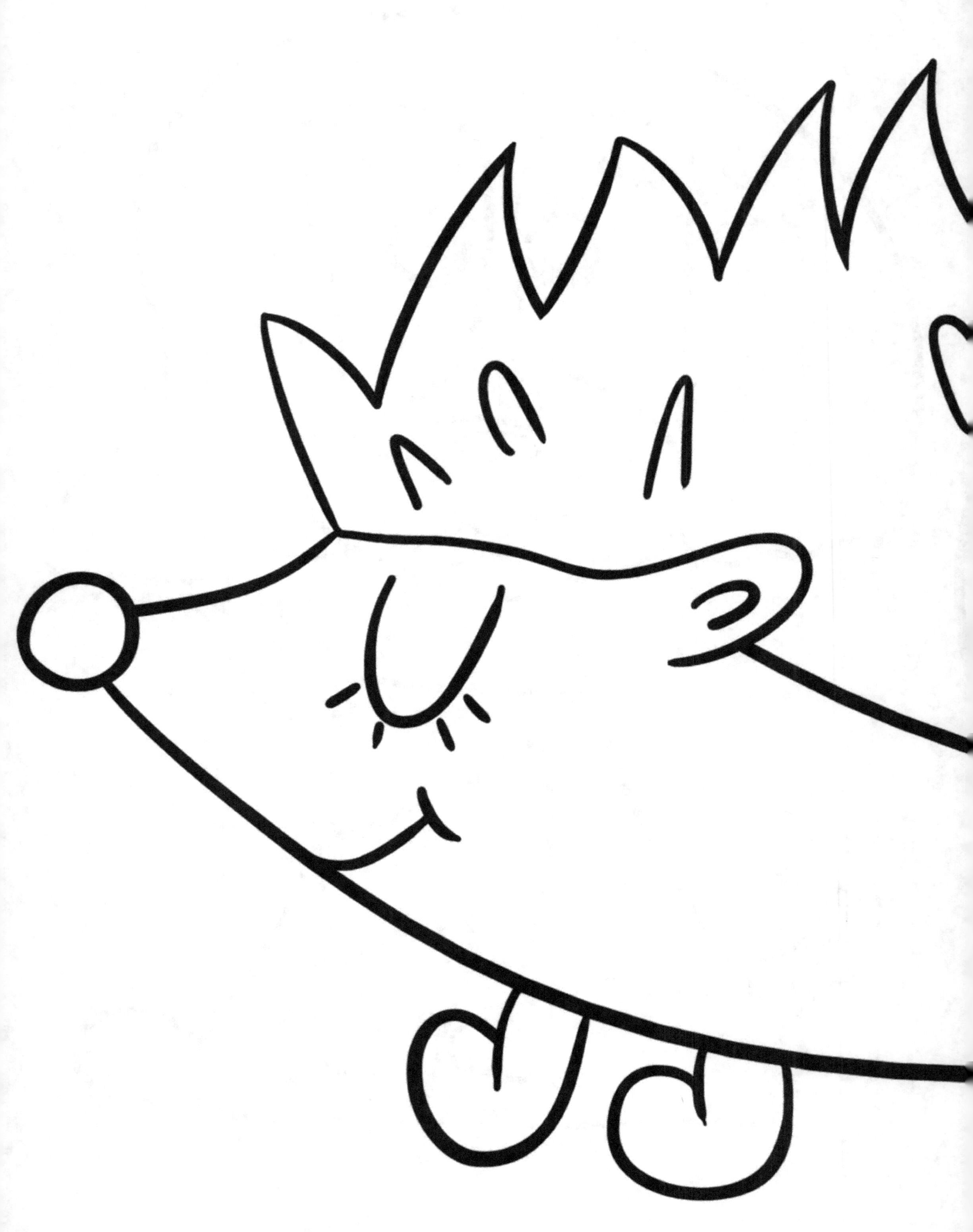

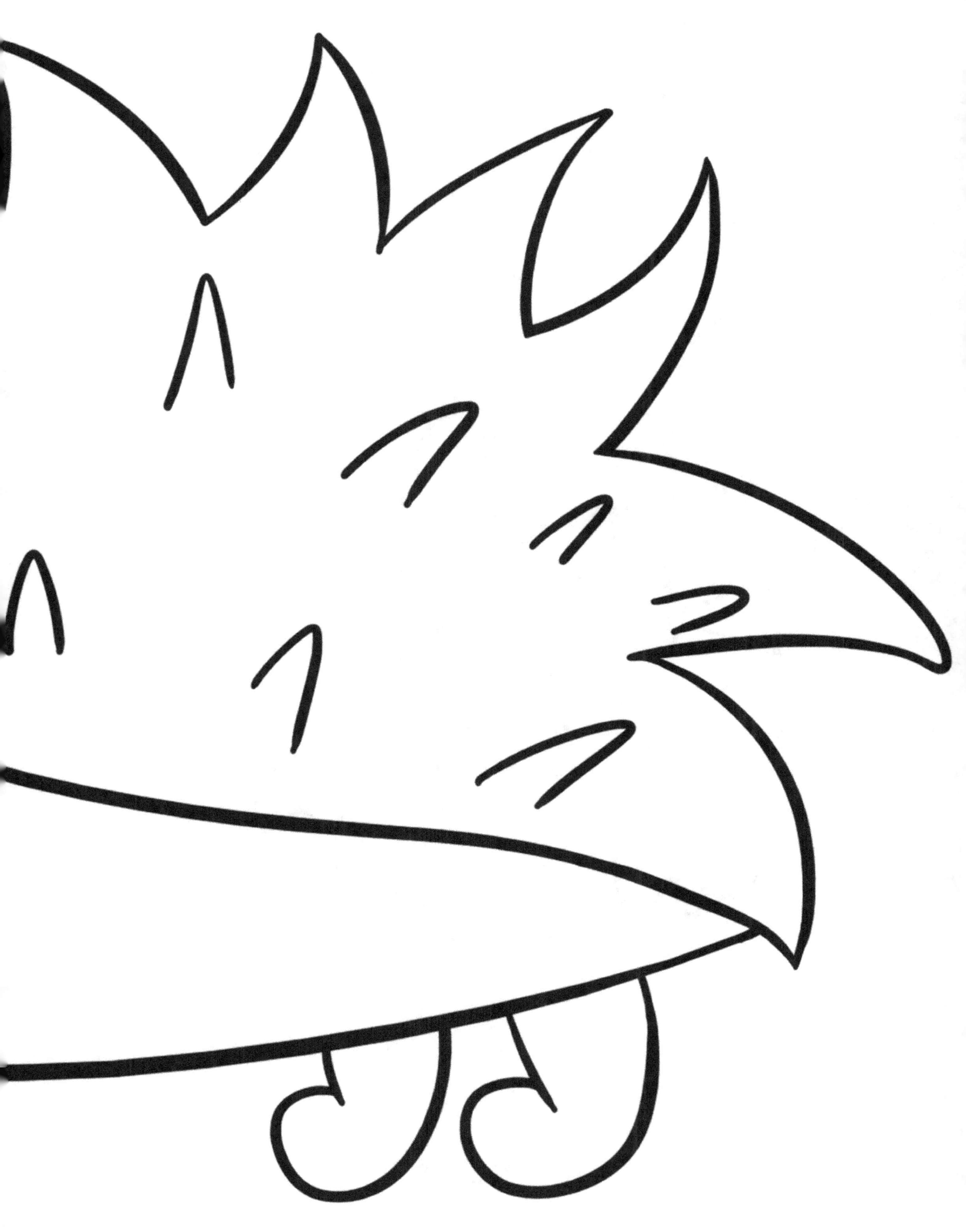

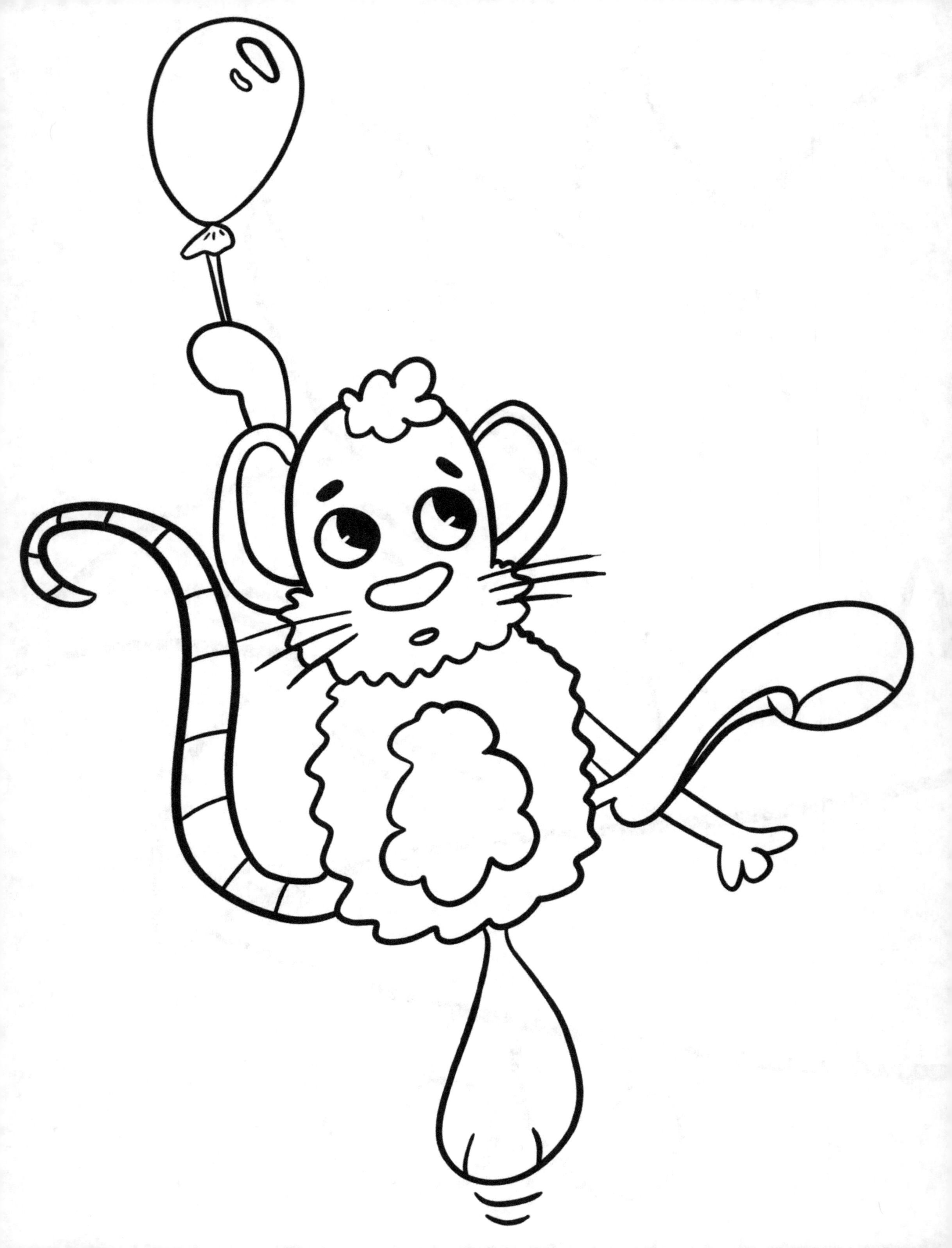

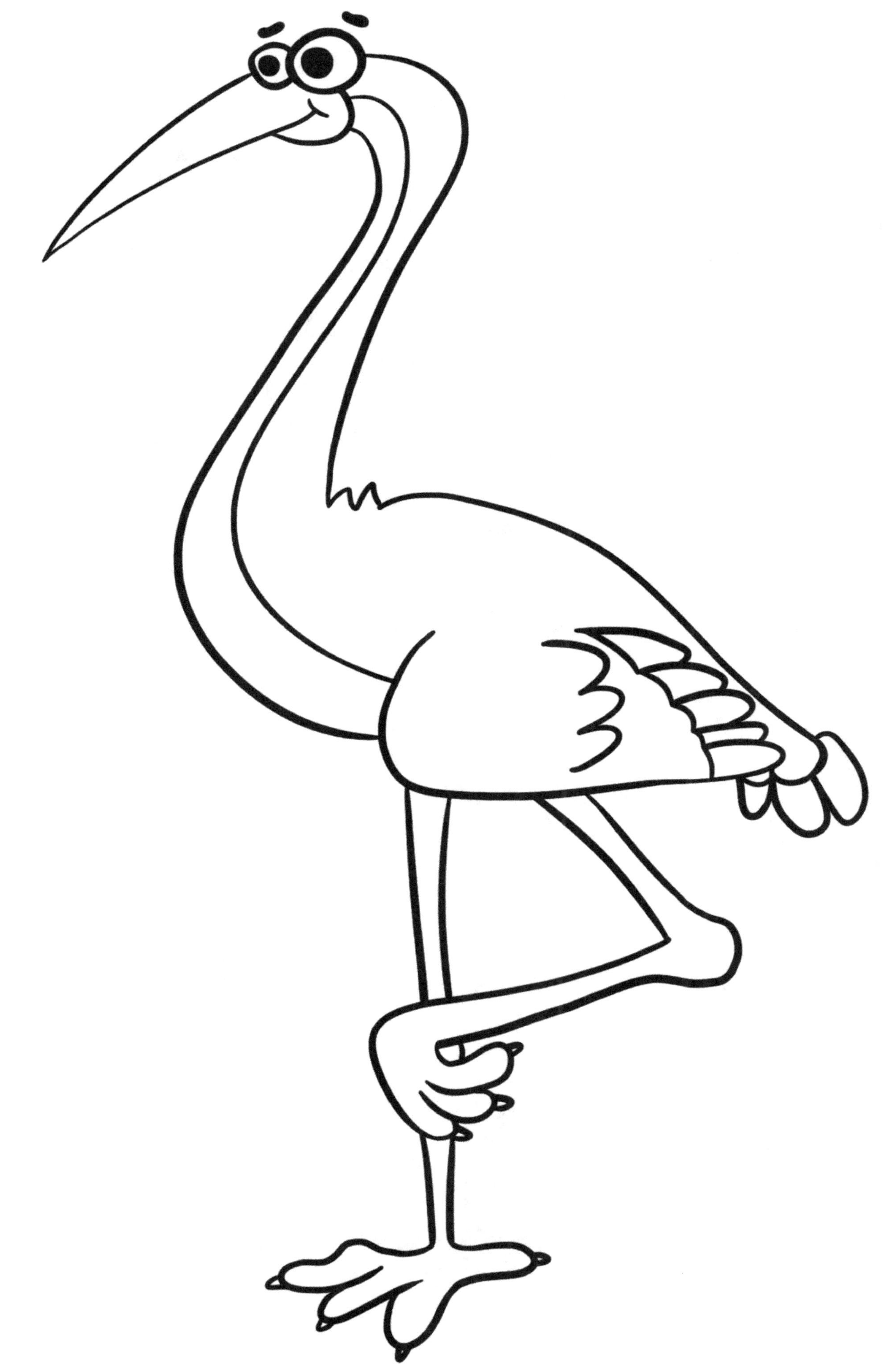

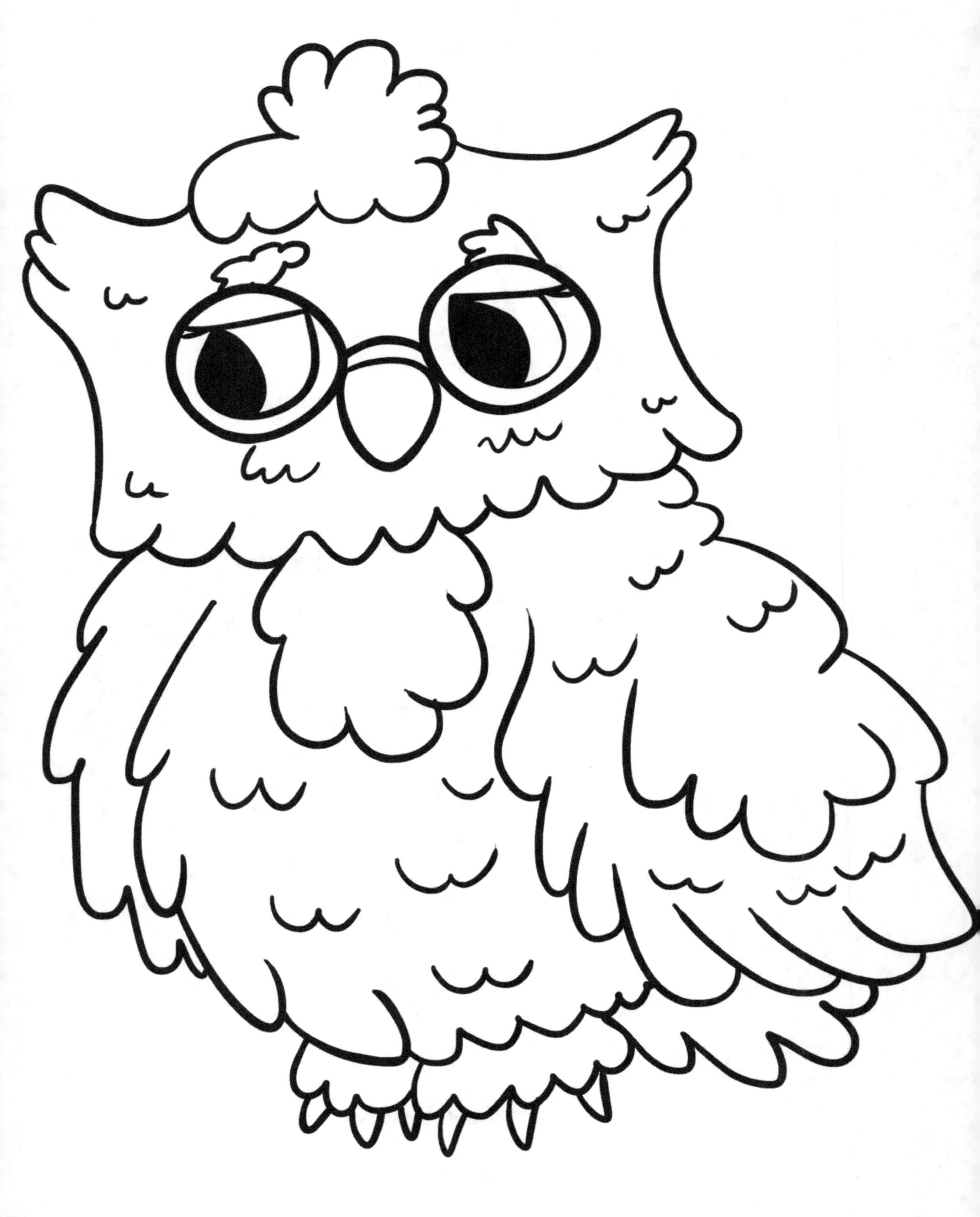

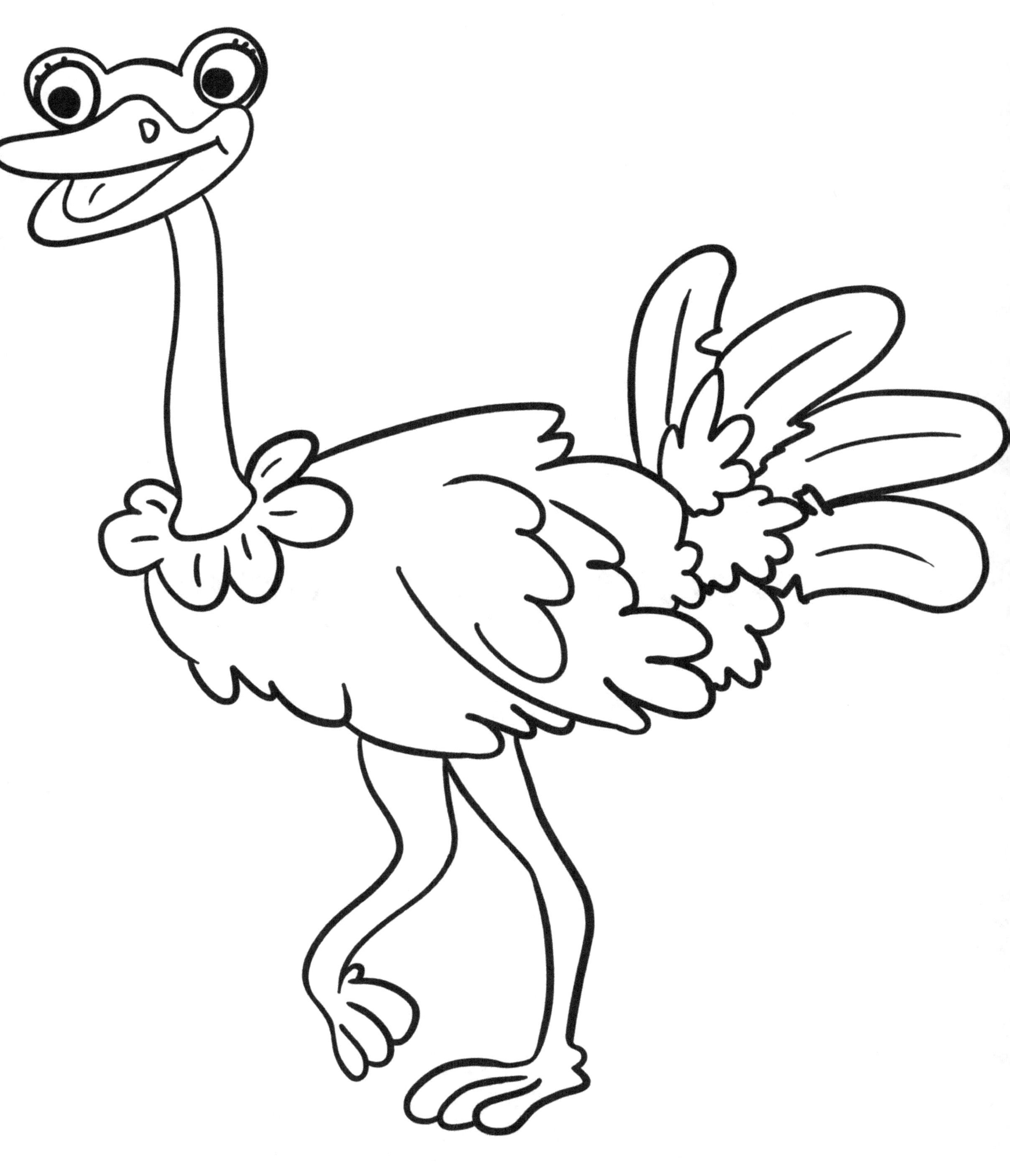

WWW.HOLZBOOKS.COM

HOLZ BOOKS